PLANET UNDER PRESSURE
POVERTY

Paul Mason

Heinemann Library
Chicago, Illinois

© 2006 Heinemann Library
a division of Reed Elsevier, Inc.
Chicago, Illinois

Customer Service 888-454-2279

Visit our website at
www.heinemannraintree.com

Editorial: Sarah Shannon
and Louise Galpine
Design: Lucy Owen and Bridge
Creative Services Ltd
Picture Research: Natalie Gray
and Sally Cole
Production: Chloe Bloom

Printed and bound in China by South
China Printing Company

10 09 08 07 06
10 9 8 7 6 5 4 3 2 1

Library of Congress Cataloging-in-Publication Data
Mason, Paul, 1967-
  Poverty / Paul Mason.
    p. cm. -- (Planet under pressure)
  Includes bibliographical references and
index.
  ISBN 1-4034-7743-4 (library binding-
hardcover : alk. paper)
  1. Poverty--Juvenile literature. I. Title. II.
Series.
  HC79.P6M375 2006
  362.5--dc22

2005017166

Acknowledgments
The publishers would like to thank the
following for permission to reproduce
copyright material: Alamy pp. **34–35**
(Bipinchandra Mistry); Christian Aid/Still
Pictures pp. **30–31** (E. Duigenan); Corbis
pp. **38–39**; Corbis pp. **20** (Robert Patrick),
26 (Benjamin Lowy); Corbis/Reuters pp.
4–5, 12–13, 42, 44, 46 (Crasto Sherwin);
Empics/EPA pp. **36–37**; Getty Images
pp.**38–39**; Mark Henley pp. **40–41**; Mary
Evans Picture Library pp. **10**; Panos pp. **6–7**
(Karen Robinson), **6–7** (Dieter Telemans),
23 (Sven Torfinn), **25** (Chien-min Chung),
31, 34–35 (Mark Henley); Reuters pp.
26–27;
Still Pictures pp. **10–11, 16–17**; Still
Pictures pp. **9** (Hartmut Schwarzbach),
22 (Nigel Dickinson), **34–35** (Shehzad
Noorani); The Granger Collection
pp. **28**; TopFoto pp. **10–11**; Trip
pp. **27** (V. Kolpakov).

Cover photographs of shanty town homes
and of homeless person and workers
reproduced with kind permission of Alamy.

Every effort has been made to contact
copyright holders of any material
reproduced in this book. Any omissions
will be rectified in subsequent printings if
notice is given to the publishers.

The paper used to print this book comes
from sustainable resources.

Dedicated to the memory of Lucy Owen

Contents

Any words appearing in the text in bold,
like this, are explained in the Glossary.

Poverty Issues Around the World

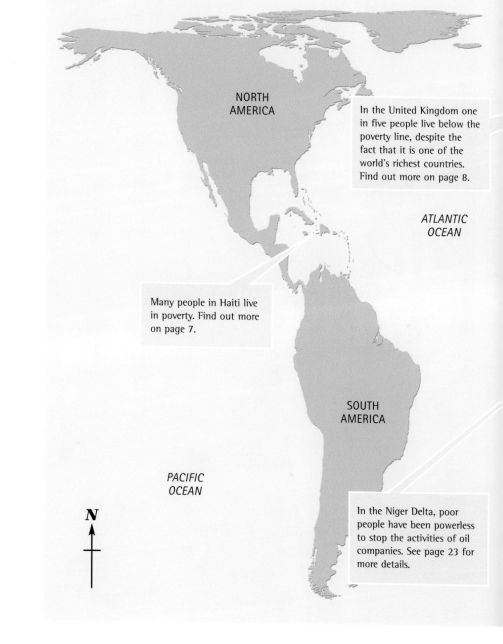

NORTH
AMERICA

In the United Kingdom one
in five people live below the
poverty line, despite the
fact that it is one of the
world's richest countries.
Find out more on page 8.

ATLANTIC
OCEAN

Many people in Haiti live
in poverty. Find out more
on page 7.

SOUTH
AMERICA

PACIFIC
OCEAN

N

In the Niger Delta, poor
people have been powerless
to stop the activities of oil
companies. See page 23 for
more details.

In Kyrzygstan, increasing numbers of people are moving to the cities. Read Zarina's story on page 27.

EUROPE

ASIA

The Grameen Bank offers loans to the poorest people—discover how and why on page 37.

In India the British took over the cotton industry, which affected the livelihoods of many Indians. Find out more on page 13.

AFRICA

The Central African Republic is one of the world's poorest countries; one of its rulers stole millions of dollars from the country. More information is on page 17.

Catastrophic floods in South Asia forced thousands of people into poverty in 2004. Details are on page 29.

AUSTRALIA

INDIAN OCEAN

What Is Poverty?

Poverty means "scarcity" or "lack." When people talk about human poverty, they usually mean a lack of some of the essentials of life. These include food, clothing, shelter, health, and education.

The international definition of poverty is based on how much money people have to live on. If they live on less than $1 per day, people are said to be living in extreme poverty. People in this position are highly unlikely to be able to feed, clothe, and shelter themselves properly. They are unlikely to be well educated, and it is often very difficult for them to educate their children. They may suffer from **malnutrition**, and probably will not live as long as those who are not living in poverty.

Children are growing up in poverty all around the world. Even in wealthy countries many children suffer from the effects of poverty.

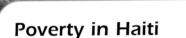

Poverty in Haiti

Haiti is one of the world's poorest countries:

- life expectancy is just 52 years
- only half of all Haitians can read
- one quarter of households have access to running water
- 123 of every 1,000 children born die before their first birthday
- the Gross National Income (GNI) per capita was just $390 in 2004
- between 1999 and 2000, Haiti became 3 percent poorer, compared to the world's other countries.

Based on the $1 per day definition of poverty, one in five of the world's people—that's 1.2 billion people—started the twenty-first century living in poverty.

This definition of poverty is based on life in the world's poorest countries. But you can buy more for a dollar in a poorer country than in a richer one. In the United States, for example, a bag of apples might cost $1. In Costa Rica, the same bag of apples might cost just 10 cents.

Most of the world's countries have developed their own poverty line. The U.S. Government, for example, set the poverty line for a single-person home at $9,827 in 2004.

Relative poverty

Relative poverty is the lack of things that most people around you have. In 2004, for example, a U.S. Census report suggested that one definition of poverty included those people who could not afford certain household appliances, new clothes, a telephone, a car, or a vacation. This was because most people in the United States *could* afford these things. Not being able to do so made people feel poor.

Yet, this definition of poverty would seem slightly ridiculous to someone living in Ethiopia, for example. In 2004, Ethiopia had 2 cars for every 1,000 people, and the GNI per person was just $110. In 2004 people lived to an average age of 44.5 years, and more than 1 baby in 10 died before its first birthday. Almost half of children under 5 years old were **undernourished**, and only about 2 of every 5 Ethiopians over 15 years old could read.

These examples make it clear that there is a big difference between relative poverty and **absolute poverty**. One way of explaining the difference is to say that relative poverty is about not having something you *want*, but can do without. Absolute poverty is linked to not having things you *need*, such as food, water, and shelter.

The Human Development Index

The Human Development Index (HDI) is one of the ways the **United Nations** measures the quality of life for people in different countries. It includes income, but also takes into account people's health and education. These are two other factors that indicate whether people are likely to be living in poverty. In 2004, the world's poorest countries, with "very low" HDI rankings, were all in Africa. The world's "very high" ranking countries were in Europe, North America, East Asia, and Australia and the Pacific islands.

Poverty in wealthy countries

"Poor people can imagine what it's like to be rich, but rich people can't imagine what it's like to be poor. My daughter went to school in shoes that cost [$8] and she came back in tears because the other kids were **taunting** her." This quote comes from someone in the United Kingdom—one of the world's wealthiest nations. Despite the fact that it is a rich country, 13 million people in the United Kingdom live below the poverty line. (The poverty line is set at 60 percent of the average **disposable income**.) This means that 6.5 million cannot afford essential winter clothes, and 9.5 million cannot afford adequate housing.

Poverty exists even in the heart of the world's most powerful economies. Homeless people begging for money are a common sight in major cities all over the developed world.

Poverty in the Past

Natural disasters, such as floods or droughts, have always been a cause of poverty. Two terrible droughts, for example, occurred during the 1870s. In India, more than five million people died as a result of a **famine** caused by drought on the Deccan Plateau. In China, more than nine million people died in a similar famine.

Poverty and the Industrial Revolution

During the 1700s and 1800s, new industries and factories began to appear in Europe and North America. People moved from the country to towns and cities, which grew rapidly. People were drawn to the cities by the promise of work in the new factories. They were also pushed from the countryside by changes in agriculture, which meant there was less work for them there.

The new industrial cities were grim, forbidding places. Living conditions were cramped, and entire families sometimes stayed in a single room. The air was often filled with pollution from the factories. People found it difficult to get clean water for drinking and cooking. Human waste, including sewage, was dumped in the rivers. In these conditions, diseases such as **cholera** and **tuberculosis** could spread quickly, killing thousands. In the United States, for example, there was a cholera **epidemic** every year between 1849 and 1866. The American Public Health Association, a national health organization, was founded as a result.

Many writers at the time of the Industrial Revolution discussed the conditions in which people lived. Novels like *Oliver Twist*, written by Charles Dickens in 1837, gave an idea of how terrible life could be for the poor—and how luxurious it was for the rich. Diseases such as cholera could infect anyone, but it was the poor in particular who were most likely to be affected.

"**Three meals of thin gruel a day, with an onion twice a week, and half a roll on Saturdays.**"
This quotation from the novel *Oliver Twist* describes the food Oliver is given to eat. (Gruel is very thin oatmeal.)

The ghost of cholera threatens figures representing the United States in the late 1800s.

Slavery

Slavery is when one human being owns another. From the 1600s to the 1800s, landowners in the Caribbean, and the United States, brought people from Africa to work as slaves on farms known as plantations. The slaves were forced to grow crops, such as cotton and sugar, which were exported to Europe and sold at high profits. The profits went to the slave-owners. Slaves continued to live in poverty.

Not only did slave-owners hold the slaves captive against their will, but some slaves were forced to work so hard that they died from exhaustion.

Imperialism and poverty

Imperialism is when one country takes over and controls another territory or country for its own benefit. During the 1800s, many European countries became imperial powers. In particular, they took over parts of Africa, South America, the Caribbean, and Asia. These regions were known as colonies.

The colonies provided European powers with raw materials such as gold, sugar, tea, or cotton. These materials were then **processed** and sold at a large profit. Sometimes they were even sold back to the colony that had provided the raw material in the first place. Most of the profit from this trade stayed in Europe, and very little went to the colonies. The colonial system kept millions of the world's non-European people poor and forced them to live in poverty.

In the 1700s and 1800s, industrialists, plantation owners, and European businessmen could become rich, while workers, slaves, and colonial peoples were forced into poverty.

Cotton in India

Beginning in the mid-1700s, the British East India Company controlled large parts of India. By this time, India's cotton industry had been producing high-quality cloth for hundreds of years. The East India Company began buying raw cotton for export to England, where it was turned into cotton cloth. The Company made it increasingly difficult for Indian cotton mills to make a profit. Soon, most of India's cotton-mill workers lost their jobs and fell into poverty. Indians were forced to buy their cloth from England, at higher prices than before.

Indian people struggled to free themselves from imperial rule by Britain. Many Indians wore clothing made in India as a sign of anti-British protest. In 1947 India became independent. Today the cotton and clothing industry is once again one of the largest employers in India.

Poverty Today

Where are people poorest?

Poverty is more common in some parts of the world than others. The map below reflects Purchasing Power Parity (PPP) dollars. These are calculated to have the same value in other countries as a dollar does in the United States. For example, if a cup of coffee costs $2 in the United States, and 6 euros in France, then 3 euros would equal 1 PPP dollar. Because it uses PPP dollars, the map shows as accurate a picture as possible of the relative wealth of different countries. The map shows that the world's poorest countries are mainly in Africa and Asia.

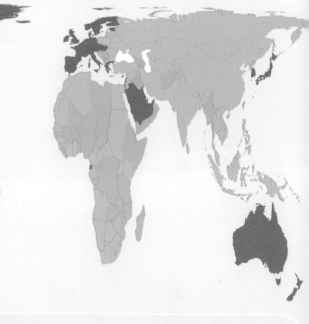

A PPP (Purchasing Power Parity) dollar has the same purchasing power in the domestic economy as $1 has in the United States.

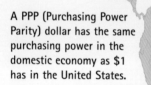

■ $10,000–$20,000

▨ $1,000–$10,000

▤ $1,000 and under

Percentage of people living on less than $1 per day:

Region	1981	2001
East Asia/Pacific	55.6	16
Europe/Central Asia	1	4
Latin America and Caribbean	10	10
Middle East/North Africa	5	2
South Asia	52	31
Sub-Saharan Africa	42	47

The effect of catastrophe

War can cause increasing numbers of people to fall into poverty. In some countries, the **GDP** per person rose or fell by 5 percent or more in the decade from 1990 to 2000. Several of these countries were in sub-Saharan Africa. There, Sierra Leone, Democratic Republic of Congo, and Burundi all experienced **civil war**. Wars make it impossible to live a normal life, and make it far more likely that people will fall into poverty. The biggest falls in GDP were in Central Asia, in countries that were once part of the **USSR**. With the break up of the USSR, they have struggled to survive alone.

Asian tigers

Most of the countries where GDP increased by more than 5 percent are in Asia and Southeast Asia. This is a reflection of the increased size of the economies of the region, some of which are known as Asian Tiger economies because of their fierce growth. Many of these countries offer international companies the chance to employ skilled workers for far lower wages than workers in Europe or North America. This outsourcing of jobs—sending them overseas—has created unemployment among former workers in wealthier countries.

Jobs, such as call-center work and textiles manufacture, have been moved from Europe and North America to Asia and India.

Who lives in poverty?

Some countries are on average much poorer than others, as the map on page 14 shows. The citizens of these poorer countries are more likely to suffer from poverty. However, poverty exists in all societies. Even in wealthy nations, some people lack the basics of life. Rich and poor exist side by side in the same country—on the same street, even. The difference between rich and poor is known as **inequality**.

As a way of measuring inequality, an Italian statistician, Corrado Gini, developed the GINI index. This measures the degree of difference between rich and poor within a country. The starting point for the GINI index is to imagine that everyone in a country has an equal share of the country's wealth. How does this compare with reality? If the rich have far more than the equal share, and the poor far less, the country gets a high GINI score. The lower a country's GINI score, the less inequality there is in that country.

Where is poverty most likely?

In countries with a high GDP and a low GINI score—for example, Scandinavian countries, such as Denmark or Sweden—there is likely to be very little poverty. The country is wealthy, and its wealth is shared equally.

Poverty is more likely in countries where the GDP is low and the GINI score is high, such as Brazil. Brazil has a middle-ranking GDP per person, but a very high GINI score. This means that much of Brazil's wealth is concentrated in the hands of a few citizens. In some countries, such as the Central African Republic (see case study), most people are very poor and the GDP per person is therefore low. Even here, though, a few powerful people sometimes manage to amass vast fortunes.

Central African Republic

Central African Republic (CAR) is one of the poorest countries in the world, with a GDP per person in 2001 of just $260. From 1966 to 1979, it was ruled by Jean-Bedel Bokassa. Despite his country's poverty, the 1977 ceremony in which Bokassa named himself Emperor was estimated to have cost about $20 million. When he was overthrown, Bokassa went into **exile** in France. He is believed to have kept millions of dollars from the sale of diamonds during his time as ruler. Bokassa returned to CAR in 1986, and in 1987 was convicted of **embezzlement** and of being an accomplice to murder.

Women, children, and poverty

Seventy percent of the world's poor are women. There are several reasons for this. Poverty is linked to women's lifestyles, the work they do, and how much they are paid.

In most societies, the job of caring for children falls to women. The time they spend feeding, clothing, and educating children often means that women can only do part-time paid work, if they can work at all. Women who are bringing up children on their own, without a husband or partner, are likely to find it even more difficult to cover their expenses.

In some parts of the world, women tended crops while men hunted for meat or fish. Today, hunting is less important, and sometimes not possible. The men have little to do, but still do not do "women's work" such as growing food. In places such as the Caribbean and some African countries, women have turned this burden into a benefit. Women take their crops to market and can earn money by selling them. Some women have created large businesses that started from a simple market stall where they sold their own produce.

WOMEN'S PAY

All around the world, women earn less than men. How much less varies from place to place: in 2000, for example, women in places as different as Denmark, Latvia, Tanzania, and Cambodia earned an average of at least 70 percent of what men earned. At the same time, though, women in Brazil, Algeria, Nigeria, and Malaysia earned on average less than half as much as men.

Partly, women earn less than men because they often work part-time. But even when women do the same jobs as men, their pay is almost always lower. This is another reason why more women than men live in poverty.

EDUCATION

Girls are often less **literate** than boys. This is especially true in societies where a woman's role is seen as being primarily a mother and housewife—an education is not believed to be useful for girls. As a result, nearly 70 percent of the world's illiterate people are women. Lack of education is linked to poverty—people who cannot read and write properly are likely to find it impossible to get a high-paying job. This has a continuing effect within a family. Mothers who cannot read or write will find it impossible to teach their children how to do so. Children who do not learn to read and write are more likely to end up living in poverty.

Educating women is essential in order to
break the cycle of poverty. Here, girls in India
are educated in basic literacy skills.

Ethnicity

The term ethnicity describes the historical and cultural background of a group of people. People from a particular ethnic group have a shared history and are originally from the same region. They have other things in common, too: their traditional clothes, food, housing, and even the stories they tell their children at bedtime. Ethnicity can be linked to poverty in several ways. One way is through wars caused by ethnic conflicts.

ETHNICITY AND CONFLICT

Rivalry between different ethnic groups can lead to conflict—sometimes armed conflict or even civil war. In recent times, there have been ethnic conflicts or civil wars in Europe (where war raged across the former Yugoslavian territories during the 1990s), in Africa (such as in Rwanda-Burundi), and in Asia (in East Timor).

The worst atrocities in Europe since World War II were committed during the Bosnian conflict in the mid-1990s. Concentration camps were set up and prisoners were tortured and murdered.

Ethnic conflicts are often accompanied by ethnic cleansing. This is a way of removing members of another ethnic group from a particular area. Large numbers of people are either forced to leave their homes or are murdered. Often the dead are left in mass graves, with hundreds of bodies piled up together. Those who are forced to leave have nowhere to live or work, and are often thrown into immediate poverty.

Wars also cause increases in poverty. Markets are disrupted, factories bombed, and railways and roads destroyed or damaged. People's lives are turned upside down, and even people far from the fighting may begin to find it increasingly difficult to make a living. Those who were already struggling to stay out of poverty may find themselves steadily sliding into it.

ETHNIC MINORITIES

The world's ethnic minorities are ethnic groups who make up only a small percentage of a country's population. They may wear a different style of clothes, cook different types of food, speak another language, or follow a different religion. They are especially likely to suffer from poverty. Discrimination against ethnic minorities means they commonly find it hard to get a good education. Their literacy and **numeracy** rates are lower than other people's, so they find it hard to get good jobs, or sometimes to get any work at all. This makes it more likely that they will suffer from poverty.

Internal refugees

In 2002, the following countries had more than 500,000 internal refugees (people who had left their homes, but stayed in the country). Those that had recently experienced civil war or serious ethnic conflict are shown in italics:

Afghanistan
Angola
Azerbaijan
Colombia
Democratic Republic of Congo
India
Iraq
Malaysia
Republic of Myanmar
Rwanda
Sierra Leone
Sudan
Syria
Turkey
Uganda

Poverty and people's environment

When people live in poverty, it often has an effect on their environment. In the short term, people use the natural **resources** around them to improve their lives. People from mountain areas, for example, may use trees for firewood. In the short term, this helps them keep warm in the winter, or even make money by selling wood. But without tree roots to hold the soil in place, the soil can be washed or blown away. New trees cannot grow without soil, and the hillsides become **barren**. The people are worse off than before. This has happened in countries as far apart as Haiti in the Caribbean, and Nepal in Asia.

Urban environments

Poverty affects urban environments, too. Areas where very poor people have built housing without permission surround many of the world's fastest-growing cities. These areas are sometimes called shanty towns. These often lack basic sewerage and **sanitation**, schools, and health care. The people living there are therefore less likely to be well-educated and healthy, making it more difficult for them to escape poverty. Cities such as Rio de Janeiro in Brazil, Lagos in Nigeria, and Dhaka in Bangladesh—among many others—all have large shanty towns.

In Rio de Janeiro, the favela, or shanty town, sits alongside the high-rise homes of the wealthy.

PROBLEMS MADE WORSE

Poor people may not be able to defend their **environment** against problems caused by others. People who have lacked educational opportunities are less likely to understand or be able to use the legal system. They will struggle to prevent pollution of rivers, the dumping of toxic waste, and the release of harmful emissions. Those living in poverty are affected by these pollution hazards more regularly than other people.

Oil in the Niger delta

Poor local people in the Niger **delta** of Nigeria have protested for years against the presence of international oil companies. They claim the oil companies are responsible for polluting the nearby land and waterways, and that the oil companies employ few local people.

Many Nigerians are also angry that much of the profit from their country's oil goes to foreign companies that sell it abroad. At the same time, Nigeria is forced to import oil from elsewhere, often a type of oil that is worse for the environment than the oil that is exported.

The Causes of Poverty

The poverty cycle is a term to describe how people become trapped in poverty. Because they are poor, it is more difficult for them to become educated and improve their standard of living than it would be otherwise. It also makes it more likely that their children will grow up poor, continuing the cycle of poverty into the next generation. They get trapped by their poverty.

Poverty cycle examples

A typical example of the poverty cycle is when children must work instead of going to school, because their family is living in poverty. The extra money they earn, even if it is only a small amount, is desperately needed. While the income helps in the short term, the children cannot go to school, and will not get an education. As a result, they will only ever be able to get low-paying jobs. When they have children of their own, the little extra money those children can earn by going out to work will again be needed. The next generation also fails to get an education, and the poverty cycle continues.

Less extreme examples of the poverty cycle occur where children do poorly in school, rather than not going to school at all. This happens most often in richer countries. There, people with low educational achievements find it hard to get work, just like illiterate people do in poorer countries.

Single-parent families and poverty

A study by UNICEF discovered that children in single-parent families in wealthy countries were at serious risk of poverty. The problem was particularly bad in the United States, Canada, and Australia, where more than 50 percent of such children were living in poverty.

In Australia, the United States, and Norway, children from single-parent families made up more than half of all children living in poverty. The reason is simple: parents (usually mothers) who are coping alone and caring for children often find it impossible to earn enough money. Only in countries with well-funded government assistance programs, such as Denmark and Sweden, do single parents get enough financial help to keep their families out of poverty.

Weaving carpets by hand is tricky work. Children have smaller, more agile fingers than adults, and many children are employed in this industry, often working in poor conditions.

Percentage of children living below the poverty line, 2000

	Children in two parent family	Children in single parent family
Australia	9	36
Belgium	4	14
Canada	10	52
Denmark	4	12
Finland	4	7
Italy	20	22
The Netherlands	7	24
Norway	2	13
Sweden	2	7
United States	16	55

The new urban poor

More and more people are leaving the countryside in search of a better life in the cities. Nearly half of the world's population now lives in cities. The largest numbers are moving from the countryside in the world's poorest regions. In Africa, the number of people living in cities is predicted to rise 14.8 percent between 2003 and 2030. In Asia, the rise is predicted to be even greater, at 15.7 percent. Meanwhile in wealthy Europe, the rise is predicted to be just 6.6 percent by 2030.

People arriving in the city from the countryside are in danger of falling into poverty. They may have nowhere to live, little money, and no job qualifications. They may find it more difficult to get work, and may quickly become trapped in the poverty cycle.

Across the developing world there are increasing numbers of abandoned villages. The occupants have left in search of a better life in the cities.

Moving to the city

Zarina lives in Kyrgyzstan, a country that was once part of the **USSR**. In 1991, Kyrgyzstan became independent. Since then, there have been tensions between the country's ethnic groups, especially between the Kyrgyz and Uzbek peoples.

In 2004, when she was 13 years old, Zarina's family sent her to live with her aunt and uncle on the outskirts of Bishkek, the capital city. They had moved there in search of a better life and better jobs, and found work in a nearby market. Earning enough money is tough, though. Her aunt, uncle, their baby, and Zarina all live in just one room, where they cook, eat, and sleep.

Zarina spends her time caring for the baby so her aunt can go to work. There is no school nearby; a school bus takes children into the city. But in any case Zarina says:

"I have to look after the baby. That's why I can't go to school!" She also says, "I would rather go to school and stay with my parents instead of looking after a baby—it is so hard because he cries a lot; now he is crawling and these things bother me. I have a few friends here, but do not have any time to play with them or to read books."

"I like to study and I did well at school, I used to get good marks."

Zarina wants to return home and continue her schooling, and hopes one day to become a history teacher. However, her family is large, with four children, and her parents may not be able to afford this. Statistics show that most children who leave school early never go back.

Poverty and vulnerability

Being vulnerable means being unable to defend yourself against attack or misfortune. Two of the most common characteristics of poverty are that poor people often lack money and education. This means that they are among the least likely to be able to defend themselves against people who *do* have money and education—such as big landowners, employers, governments, and large international companies.

Around the world there have been many examples of poor people being mistreated by those more powerful than them. Settlers, ranchers, or miners have slowly pushed **indigenous** peoples off their land. In Brazil, for example, native peoples of the Amazon have lost land to ranchers, loggers, and new settlers. In southern Africa, the San people have seen the land they have used for centuries fenced off by cattle farmers.

Elsewhere, people lose their land to local moneylenders who charge very high interest rates. Everywhere, it is usually the poor who end up working the longest hours in the worst conditions.

In 1838 and 1839, the Cherokee nation was forced to move to new lands in Oklahoma. The Cherokee people called this journey the "Trail of Tears." More than 4,000 Cherokees died during the migration.

After major floods hit India, the people there face an uncertain future. With little money, it will not be easy for them to recover from such a catastrophe.

Floods in South Asia

Because they do not have money saved, poor people are less likely to be able to recover from sudden disasters such as flooding, volcanic eruptions, or hurricanes.

In 2004, severe flooding affected large areas of South Asia. Thousands of people were left homeless, without food, clean water, or shelter. In Bangladesh, three million people were left marooned by floodwater. At least 50 people were killed by flash floods in Nepal. In Assam, India, Chief Minister Tarun Gogoi said:

"This is the worst flooding in recent memory, with 22 of the 24 districts in Assam under floodwater. The high water current has washed away rows and rows of villages. The condition of the people is really devastating."

Many of the people in this region are extremely poor. They do not have savings or insurance, and are likely to feel the effects of the floods for many years to come. Some will be pushed permanently into a state of poverty.

FINANCIAL CHANGES

By definition, people on the edge of poverty have little or no money to spare. They are unlikely to be able to cover all their living expenses. Changes in the amount of money they need to spend can have a drastic effect. If, for example, food prices rise by a small amount, this may be enough to mean that poor people can no longer afford their rent. They risk becoming homeless.

Similarly, if the amount of money coming in to a household falls, this can have a terrible effect. Losing a job, a reduction in welfare payments, or even a short illness that means time off work—each of these can tip a person or family on the brink of poverty over the edge.

Population size and poverty

Statistically, there is a link between population size and poverty. Family sizes are growing fastest in the world's poorest regions. The highest rates of increase in population are in sub-Saharan Africa and Asia. In Nigeria, for example, 55 percent of the population was under nineteen years old in 2000. By contrast, in parts of wealthy Europe the population is actually decreasing, as more people die than are born.

THE IDEAS OF THOMAS MALTHUS

Some experts have suggested that large population size and rapid population growth are among the causes of poverty. This idea dates back to an eighteenth-century British economist named Thomas Malthus. Malthus' idea was that population increased at a faster rate than food resources. If the population continued to grow, he argued that one day there would no longer be enough resources to go around. Malthus theorized that poverty and wars would keep the population in check, as people competed for the resources that were available.

In the 1960s and 1970s, Malthus' ideas were often used to explain poverty. Effectively, people argued that the poor lived in poverty because they had so many children to feed. Controlling population growth was seen as the best way to reduce poverty. Having fewer children to feed would mean there was more food to go around.

FOOD SUPPLY AND POPULATION INCREASE

The problem with Malthusian theories was that they do not completely fit the facts. Between 1960 and 2000, the world's population increased by 100 percent to 6 billion people. At the same time, the world's food supply increased by just 20 percent. Yet great progress was made in reducing poverty. Around the world, more people became literate; people lived longer, were better fed, and had better housing. Experts began to suggest that rather than being poor because they had large families, people had large families because they were poor. They began to think poor families were choosing to have large numbers of children.

CHOOSING A LARGE FAMILY

Poor people might choose to have large families for several reasons. Children born into poverty are less likely to survive, causing some families to have more children than they would ideally like. If parents feel some of their children may not survive, they may have more. Children's income is valuable to parents—in some countries, a 12-year-old can earn as much as an adult. Finally, in countries where there is no government care for the elderly it can be important to have children who will care for their parents when they are old.

CONTRACEPTION

Contraception is taking deliberate action to prevent pregnancy. In some countries, women do not have access to information on contraception because they cannot read. Even if they are able to obtain methods of contraception, they may not use them properly because they are unable to read the instructions. This increases the chances of women becoming pregnant even when they may not wish to.

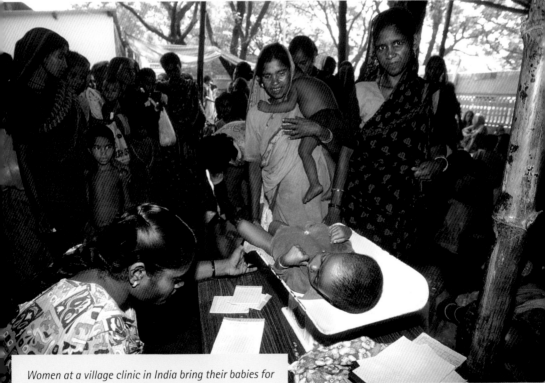

Women at a village clinic in India bring their babies for a medical check-up. The children are weighed to determine if they are developing normally.

The debt mountain

Most people living in absolute poverty live in the world's poorer countries. Why do their governments not provide the schools, health-care facilities, and work-training programs that could help get people out of poverty? Part of the answer is that the government may have to spend its money to pay back international debts.

These international debts are a result of loans that often date from the late 1960s and 1970s. Banks and other organizations lent large sums to the governments of poorer countries, many of them in Central and South America, Africa, and Asia. The money was often spent on large projects, such as dams or military equipment. Sometimes it disappeared into the pockets of **corrupt** officials. Only occasionally did it lead to improving the lives of ordinary citizens.

Many lobby groups around the world campaign to have the debts of poor countries written off or cancelled forever.

Today the governments of many poor countries still have to pay back these debts. By 2000, the debts owed by the world's poorer countries had reached the large sum of nearly $2 trillion. This is why the debt situation is sometimes called the debt mountain.

Many debts have grown so large that they can never be paid back, even though the amount of the original loan has by now been repaid several times over. The poorer countries can only pay the **interest** on these debts. This takes up a large proportion of the foreign currency they earn through trade. Little or nothing is left for helping people climb out of poverty.

Foreign aid

Richer countries do try to help by giving poorer countries aid payments. These are designed to help raise the standard of living. Aid payments sometimes come with strings attached, though. Many are made in the form of loans. Others are tied to specific projects, such as dam building, on the understanding that the aid-giving country will profit from the project. Very few countries receive more in aid than they pay out on their debts.

The amount of aid richer countries give varies. According to the UN's *Human Development Report*, in 2000 Denmark was the most generous, giving $348 in aid from every man, woman, and child. Greece was least generous, giving $25 per person. The amount of aid given can also be expressed as a percentage of national income. By this measure, the United States was the least generous aid-giver in 2000. The United States gave just 0.1 percent of its national income, or $35 per person.

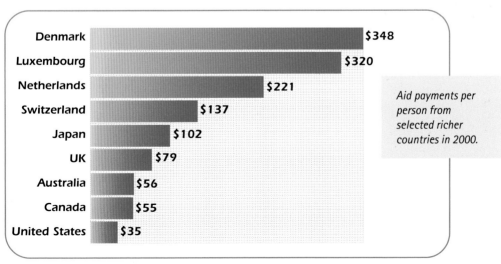

Aid payments per person from selected richer countries in 2000.

Globalization has led to the mixing of cultures. Here a young Japanese girl, dressed in a traditional kimono, eats a burger in an international fast food chain's restaurant.

Globalization

Globalization describes the process of people beginning to think and act in a similar way all around the world. One way this happens is through TV. Shows, such as *Friends,* are broadcast globally. These shows feature fashionable clothes, comfortable apartments, plenty of free time, and no shortage of food. Viewers everywhere start to feel that they want this lifestyle for themselves. The Internet is another powerful tool for the globalization of ideas. Globalization of this kind has been responsible for an increase in relative poverty—people who are not in absolute poverty, but feel relatively poor.

Globalization also describes the way businesses or companies operate internationally. For example, car manufacturers, drink manufacturers, or fast food restaurants may operate in many different countries. Such companies are often called Trans-National Corporations (TNCs). Famous TNCs include Coca-Cola, Starbucks, Nike, and General Motors. TNCs often have manufacturing and distribution operations spread all round the world.

BENEFITS OF GLOBALIZATION

Globalization can bring benefits to poorer countries. If a large TNC decides to open a manufacturing plant in Indonesia, for example, the plant may employ hundreds or thousands of local people. The money the workers earn is spread out through the economy, as it is spent on clothes, food, cars, and other goods.

The globalization of ideas can also be a good thing. Through it, people can learn the benefits of ideas from different cultures, such as women's rights, cultural diversity, and democracy.

GLOBALIZATION NEGATIVES

Some critics claim globalization adds to world poverty. They point out that TNCs open factories in poorer countries to make more money—the cost of factory workers in Indonesia is less than in the United States or the United Kingdom. Moving production to poorer countries takes jobs away from other workers and creates poverty. People also argue that little of the money paid to workers in poorer countries ends up helping the poverty-stricken. Instead it goes to the skilled workers who are employed in such factories.

Some people also see the globalization of ideas as a bad thing. They argue that as more and more people hold Western-based ideas, it becomes harder for anyone else to think differently. People can become **marginalized**, and cut off from the benefits that can go with the new globalized way of thinking.

Tackling Poverty

There has always been a small group of people who never manage to escape from poverty. They may have become dependent on welfare payments where these were available, or simply have been people who lacked the ability to work. The media pay a lot of attention to this group of poor people, and it can be tempting to view people who live in poverty as doing nothing to try to escape from their current existence. But most people who live in poverty lack only the opportunity to help themselves. Given the chance, they will work as hard as possible to make a better life.

Various initiatives have been set up to help the homeless. In many cities, homeless people sell magazines to earn money.

The Big Issue

Around the world, a number of programs have been developed to help people escape from poverty. In 1991, the *Big Issue* magazine was started in the United Kingdom. Homeless people buy the magazines from the publisher at 40-50 percent of the cover price and sell it on the street. The profit provides much-needed money through work instead of begging. The magazine now has editions in Australia, the United States, and South Africa.

Micro-credit programs

Around the world, micro-credit programs have helped millions of people escape poverty. The first of these was the Grameen Bank, which was started in 1976 in Bangladesh. Such programs make small loans to poor people to help them start a business without having to go to moneylenders who will charge them high interest.

Micro-credit programs were so successful in poorer countries that they are now also being used elsewhere. Washington and Illinois have micro-credit programs. One of the great achievements of micro-credit is that it allows people to feel proud of having pulled themselves out of poverty.

The Grameen Bank

Founded in 1976 in Bangladesh, the Grameen Bank now has almost 3.7 million members—quite a jump from the original 42!

The Grameen Bank works on trust, taking people's word that they will pay their debts. Members make regular deposits with the bank as well as borrowing. Many of the members are women—as well as being the poorest people in many societies, they tend to invest more of their money in their children. This makes it doubly unlikely that their children will grow up in poverty.

The international community

The international community has agreed on a set of goals for reducing poverty. These goals are all supposed to be reached by 2015. The goals include to:

- reduce by half the number of people living in absolute poverty between 1990 and 2015
- reduce by two-thirds the death rate among children under the age of five
- make sure that all children are going at least to primary school
- make sure that boys and girls have equal opportunities for an education.

Governments are supposed to be working towards these targets. With less than ten years to go, though, it is beginning to look unlikely that they will be reached in time.

A speaker addresses an international audience, represented by the world flags behind him. International meetings and treaties are seen by many as a valuable tool in eradicating poverty.

Reducing the debt mountain

One way to help the governments of poor countries could be to reduce their debt payments. Some argue that all debts should be forgotten. This is rarely possible, but the HIPC (Heavily Indebted Poor Countries) Initiative tries to help poor countries cope better with their debts. The HIPC attempts to get the poorest countries' debt payments set at a lower level. The idea is that the payments should not be so high that they affect the government's chances of helping people out of poverty. Most of the countries in the HIPC are in sub-Saharan Africa; a few are in Central and South America.

The World Bank

The World Bank is linked to the United Nations. It makes loans to countries for development projects like housing, irrigation plans, and education initiatives. Part of the World Bank, called the International Development Association, also makes **interest**-free loans to the poorest countries.

The IMF

The IMF (International Monetary Fund) is connected to the World Bank. It makes short-term loans to member countries. Often the IMF insists on spending cuts by a government before it will lend them money. Anti-poverty groups have criticized this—they say the spending cuts often affect education, health care, and **social security**, and push more people into poverty.

Aid payments

The United Nations has agreed that richer countries should give 0.7 percent of their national income to poorer countries. This money would help poorer nations make a better life for their people and reduce poverty. But in 2004, only Denmark, Norway, Sweden, Luxembourg, and The Netherlands managed to give 0.7 percent or more.

Poverty Tomorrow

Individuals, groups of people, charities, governments, and international organizations all work to reduce poverty. There have been improvements in recent decades. More people than ever before have access to modern health care, schools, and decent living conditions. The percentage of the world's population living on less than $1 a day fell from 30 percent in 1990 to 21 percent in 2001. How can poverty be reduced even more?

The rich-poor divide

The rich-poor divide is the name for the gap in living standards between the best-off and the least well-off people in a country. Some of the world's poorest countries, where absolute poverty is worst, also have the greatest differences between rich and poor. If ways can be found of lessening this difference, it usually means poor people are escaping poverty.

Redistribution of wealth

In Scandinavian countries, such as Denmark, for example, higher taxes on those who earn a lot are used to support a generous welfare system. Payments from this system help to keep high educational standards and good health care. They also provide money to people who do not earn enough, keeping them from poverty.

Population controls

The relationship between poverty and population growth is complicated. However, it is clear that a growing population will make greater demands on health care, education, and housing resources. The world's population is expanding rapidly, especially in poorer countries. It is forecast to increase by 50 percent, reaching 9 billion, by 2050. This means that the resources currently available will not be adequate.

Economic development

Countries such as China have been able to improve the living standards of citizens despite an expanding population. One way China has done this is by limiting the number of children people are allowed. Another is by establishing a government plan for how industries will develop in specific places. Sometimes this has meant relocating entire towns so that there will be enough workers available in a particular area.

India, too, has raised living standards despite a growing population. Various Trans National Companies have moved some of their operations to India. Countries such as China, India, Thailand, and South Korea have all benefited from moves by TNCs to locate their businesses where labor is cheaper. Often this has meant factories, call centers, and other employers have been closed down in richer countries. However, these richer countries are often the very places where there is a welfare system that can help people stay out of poverty.

China's economy is developing very quickly. Cities, such as Shanghai (above), have seen a boom in building and construction as foreign businesses have moved into this new market.

Statistical Information

Countries where 80 percent of the population was living on less than $2 per day in 2004 (where figures available).

Region	Affected countries
Latin America	Nicaragua
Africa	The Gambia, Mali, Burkina Faso, Niger, Nigeria, Central African Republic, Uganda, Rwanda, Zambia, Madagascar
Asia	India, Nepal, Bangladesh, Pakistan

GDP (2004) and GINI (2002) rating for various countries

Country	GDP per person in $	GINI rating
Australia	30,448	35.2
Bangladesh	1,910	33.6
Brazil	8,016	60.7
Central African Republic	1,002	61.3
China	5,559	40.3
Denmark	32,106	24.7
France	28,636	32.7
Haiti	1,483	–
India	3,072	37.8
Kyrgyz Republic	1,651	34.6
New Zealand	22,927	–
Nicaragua	2,258	60.3
Nigeria	976	50.6
Russian Federation	9,817	48.7
Switzerland	33,635	33.1
United Kingdom	29,483	36.8
United States	39,731	40.8
Vietnam	2,720	36.1

GDP per person describes the average wealth per person in a country; these GDP per person figures are adjusted for Purchasing Power Parity, meaning they give an idea of relative wealth between countries. A country's GINI rating describes the level of inequality, with a score of 0 meaning there is no inequality.

Personal wealth is sometimes indicated by the number of consumer products people can afford, especially high-tech products such as computers.

Country	Number of personal computers per 1,000 people, 2001	Number of phone lines per 1,000 people, 2001
Afghanistan	–	1
Australia	516	541
Bangladesh	2	4
Brazil	63	218
Central African Republic	2	2
China*	19	137
Denmark	541	721
France	329	574
Haiti	–	10
India	6	38
Kyrgyz Republic	13	78
New Zealand	393	477
Nicaragua	25	30
Nigeria	7	5
Russian Federation	75	243
Switzerland	681	743
United Kingdom	366	594
United States	625	671
Vietnam	9	38

*excludes Chinese territories of Hong Kong and Macao.

A 2004 UNICEF report showed that more than half the world's children are suffering extreme deprivations from poverty, war, and HIV/AIDS.

640 million children did not have adequate shelter

500 million children had no access to sanitation

400 million children did not have access to safe water

300 million children lacked access to information

270 million children had no access to health care services

140 million children had never been to school

90 million children were severely food-deprived.

Glossary

absolute poverty poverty that is not relative; under any circumstances it would be regarded as poverty

barren infertile; area where crops cannot be grown

cholera highly infectious disease that comes from contaminated food or water and causes vomiting, diarrhea, and death. Cholera spreads quickly in crowded conditions, which are most common among the poorest people.

civil war war between different groups of people who live in the same country

corrupt not honest or pure

delta wetland area at the mouth of a river

disposable income amount of money people have left over after they have paid for their food, clothing, and shelter.

embezzlement taking money that belongs to an organization, such as a country or business, for your personal use

environment physical surroundings

epidemic outbreak of disease that spreads more quickly and more widely than expected

exile being forced to leave your own country

famine widespread shortage of food that results in hunger and starvation

GDP stands for Gross Domestic Product. The GDP is the total value of goods and services provided within a country during one year.

GNI stands for Gross National Income. The GNI per person is the GNI divided by the population size. This is a way of showing the average income in a country, although most people earn either more or less than the GNI per person.

indigenous local, or coming from an area. Native Americans, for example, are indigenous to the United States.

inequality describes something that is not equal or fair

interest cost of borrowing money. It is usually expressed as a percentage. So 3 percent interest on a loan of $1 billion would be $3 million per year.

literacy/literate ability to read and write

malnutrition condition in which the body is not supplied with proper nutrients, due to lack of food or disease, leading to poor health and possibly death

marginalized away from the center of power and influence. People who are marginalized typically find it more difficult to get access to education, health care, and government aid.

numeracy ability to use numbers

processed product that has been worked on to change it in some way. For example, a frozen pizza bought from a store has been processed.

relative poverty poverty within a context. Depending on the situation, it might not be seen as poverty. It is only poverty viewed in the context of its surroundings.

resources supply of something, such as energy, money, or raw materials

sanitation cleanliness, such as being able to take a bath or shower

social security government payments to help people who cannot support themselves, for example, if they are ill or unemployed. Also referred to as welfare or government aid.

taunting teasing in a hurtful or cruel way

tuberculosis highly infectious disease of the lungs that causes death unless it is properly treated. Until the late 1800s there was no cure for tuberculosis.

undernourished without enough food to eat

UNICEF United Nations Children's Fund United Nations organization concerned with children's welfare

United Nations (UN) international organization in which the world's governments work together to try to deal with issues, such as poverty

USSR Union of Soviet Socialist Republics, which until 1990 rivaled the United States as the world's most powerful country. When the USSR split up in 1991, many of the republics declared themselves independent. Some are still grouped together as the Commonwealth of Independent States (CIS).

Further Reading

Books

Bowden, Rob. *Food Supply*. Chicago: Raintree-Heinemann, 2003.
A guide to the food industry and food distribution around the world, this book gives information about how and why those living in poverty fail to get enough to eat.

Bowden, Rob. *Just the Facts: World Poverty*. Chicago: Raintree-Heinemann, 2003.
This is an excellent examination of the history and global causes of poverty.

Gresser, Charis, and Sophia Tickell. *Mugged: Poverty In Your Coffee Cup*. Oxford: Oxfam, 2004.
This book looks at what goes into your morning cup of coffee, including a look at who wins and who loses from the international trade in coffee.

Stearman, Kaye, Emma Haughton, Fiona MacDonald. *World Issues: Poverty*. London: Chrysalis Children's Books, 2002.
In this book learn how poverty is a global issue.

An adult can help you with these books:
Smith, Dan. *The State of the World Atlas*. New York: Penguin, 2003.
An invaluable, map-based graphic presentation of facts and figures under such headings as Power, Cost of Living, Rights, War and Force, Money, and Life and Death, this book provides comparisons between different parts of the world, interesting statistics, and text explaining the facts in short, easily understood bursts. It is regularly reprinted and updated.

The World Bank, *Mini Atlas of Global Development*. The World Bank, 2004.
Under the headings People, Health, Economy, Environment, and Global Links, this pocket-sized book contains a world of information. Do you want to know how many people in China have personal computers, or in which countries less than half the population can read? You'll find out here.

Websites

ActionAid
www.actionaid.org
Working in over 30 countries, with more than 6 million of the world's poorest people, ActionAid is dedicated to creating a world without poverty. "Actionzone" is a special link for youth action on poverty.

Grameen Bank
www.grameen-info.org
This website of the Grameen Bank organization includes information on its new projects to help the poor in Bangladesh and around the world.

Jubilee 2000
www.jubileeplus.org
The Jubilee 2000 campaign tries to eliminate debts for poor countries.

Oxfam International
www.oxfam.org
Oxfam is one of the oldest organizations campaigning and working against poverty. Follow the links to visit their country sites around the world.

United Nations Schools Site
www.un.org/cyberschoolbus
Learn about development and the work of the United Nations.

United States Agency for International Development (USAID)
www.usaid.gov
USAID is the United States' main provider of aid and poverty assistance overseas.

World Bank Poverty Net
www.worldbank.org/poverty
This is one of the best sites for understanding more about poverty. It includes basic- and advanced-level information.

Index